Missing

People

Unusual Missing Persons Cases, Reports And The True Stories Of Missing People

Ryan Gillmore

Ryan Gillmore

Table of Contents

Want more books?

Would you love books delivered straight to your inbox every week?

Free?

How about non-fiction books on all kinds of subjects?

We send out e-books to our loyal subscribers every week to download and enjoy!

All you have to do is join! It's so easy!

Just visit the link at the end of this book to sign up and then wait for your books to arrive!

Introduction

I want to thank you and congratulate you for purchasing the book, *"Missing People: Unusual Missing Persons Cases, Reports And The True Stories Of Missing People"*.

5 years, 10, 15 or 50-- it doesn't matter how many years have gone by-- if you have a loved one who went missing and never returned, each year can be torture. The moment the news of a disappearance has spread, people will start giving you clues, leads will overflow, and suspicions will pour out. Even if you take each of the tips seriously, it's not a guarantee that you will be reunited with your loved one.

Disappearance cases are always stressful. In the cases we will discuss in this book, you will realize that one detail from the past can make a brother suspect his sister. You will notice that even though the leads are abundant, most of them are vague: incapable of pointing you in the right direction. The case could have happened almost 8 decades ago, but a new lead will emerge. Ordinary people, no matter how simply they live, can always have something sinister come upon them.

Thanks again for purchasing this book, I hope you enjoy it!

Chapter 1: The Missing Trio

Three girls who went out Christmas shopping on December 23, 1974, went missing and never returned. What happened to this mystery that has been a cold case for over 40 years?

2 days before Christmas of 1974, married high school student, and 17 year old Rachel Trlica, picked up her girlfriend Renee Wilson who was, at that time, 14 years old. According to some accounts from Renee's family, Renee probably didn't plan on going anywhere, but since Rachel invited her and she had a car (an Oldsmobile '98), she agreed to go Christmas shopping.

They went to *Seminary South Shopping Center* (it's now called *Forth Worth Town Center*) in South Fort Worth and then return home at around 4:00pm in the afternoon. Before they left, the 9-year old girl, Julie Mosely, who lived across from Rachel's grandmother's house, begged to come along with them. The older girls agreed (even though according to reports, Rachel didn't personally know Julie).

They told Julie that she had to get permission from her mother. Not wanting to stay in the house alone, Julie convinced her mom to let her go. Thinking no danger would fall upon her young daughter, Rayanne Mosely, Julie's mother, agreed to her plea.

Rachel was a Caucasian female with a brown-going-blonde hair color. Her eyes were blue-green. Rachel's front tooth was chipped and on her chin, she had a small scar. Since she was married, Rachel was wearing a wedding ring at the time of her disappearance. Renee, on the other hand wore purple/blue pants, a yellow-green t-shirt with *"Sweet Honesty"* print, and red and white sneakers.

Like Rachel, she also wore a promise ring, given to her by Julie's older brother who was at that time, Renee's crush. Julie had blue eyes and light brown hair. She had three identifying scars on her body: one under her left eye, one at the center of her forehead, and the other one on her calf.

On that afternoon, the three girls went to *Army Navy* store to collect the gifts that were in the layaway. After that, they went straight to the mall and parked the car in the upper parking lot near *Sears*. When some patrons of the mall were interviewed, they said that they saw the girls and even remembered Renee's *"Sweet Honesty"* t-shirt.

The police searched for the car they used and at 6:00 pm

on the same day, they found it locked in the parking lot. The authorities assumed that they went back to their vehicle safely because the shopping bags were safe inside. The girls, however, were nowhere to be seen.

Since the girls were not yet missing for long, the police still assumed that they just went somewhere and failed to give notice to their families. And as if to side with the police suspicion, a letter arrived in the Trlica Residence on December 24. It was addressed to Thomas A. Trlica, who was Rachel's husband, and it was written with Rachel's name on the upper-left corner.

The letter was also odd, to say the least. It bore no city on the postmark and the "3" in the postal service number 76083 was written backwards. For investigator Dan James, it could be that the last two digits of the numbers were hand-loaded. Perhaps it was really "76038" which would make the letter come from Eliasville, near Thockmorton. If the last digit was an unfinished "8", then it came from Weatherford. The letter said:

"I know I'm going to catch it, but we just had to get away. We're going to Houston, see you in about a week. The car is in Sear's upper lot. Love, Rachel."

On top of these observations, police said that the letter was written in a childish manner. For instance, the "L" in

Rachel was shorter that it resembled an "e". Whoever wrote the letter, went back to make the "L" longer.

For Thomas and Rachel's family, the suspicious letter was not written by their loved one. A dead give away for them was how Rachel referred to Thomas using his whole name. Thomas said that Rachel always called him "Tommy" and she was almost always never formal with him.

Frustrated because the families were now falling apart, the involved parties hired a private investigator named Jon Swain. The detective was described as "flamboyant" and he demanded the case files to be provided to him by the police. He called conferences and began placing headlights on the case, as well as himself. Throughout his "investigation", he received various tips that offered the whereabouts of the girls' bodies, but each time it turned out to be a hoax.

He even said that an "unidentified" man kept calling him, asking for reward money in exchange for info he could give about the girls. John Swain died in 1979 and the police ruled it as suicide. All his case files about the missing girls were lost, but the families doubted if he ever uncovered anything at all. This was because all of John Swain's leads pointed them to nothing.

For example: he received an anonymous call which told him that the girls' bodies could be found near Port Lavaca. Even before this tip, the police had already assigned few people and searched the area but they found nothing. This time, with John's enthusiasm, he urged the police to assign a hundred people. Despite the enormous number of volunteers, not one body was located.

Other examples were what happened in the year 1975 and 1976. In 1975, skeletal remains of a woman and a girl were found near San Antonio, but when the police inspected, they did not belong to any of the three girls. In 1976, a tip was received that the girls were in an oil well. Although no particular oil well was mentioned, the police searched the small community of Rising Star near Abilene since there were oil wells there. No bodies were recovered.

More than two decades later, foul play by a loved one was also looked into, particularly, one that involved Rachel's sister, Debra. According to the family history, Thomas was first engaged to Debra before he married Rachel. When interviewed about this issue, Debra insisted that the engagement was not a serious one. It was when they had a sort-of falling out, that Thomas dated Rachel.

Shortly before the disappearance of the girls, Debra had a row with her boyfriend, so she stayed with the then newly wedded Trlica couple. According to Thomas and Debra, there was no awkwardness in that situation. He and Debra long agreed that their romantic relationship was solidly over. In fact, Rachel even invited her to join them in their shopping, but she declined because she wanted to stay in bed the whole day.

Despite these believable explanations, the families of the missing girls still suspected that Debra knew more than she was letting on. They asked her to divulge all the info she had. Debra admitted that even her brother, Rusty (who was only 11 at the time of the disappearance), believed that she was the one who wrote the letter. Debra insisted that she knew nothing about the disappearance.

Her only theory was that the girls were taken to be "white slaves". The case, even though it happened 26 years ago at the time of the feud, clearly created a gap between Debra and her brother, Rusty. This is very unfortunate, considering the fact that the two grew up to be "allies".

In fact, at the start of Rachel's disappearance, the two would often find themselves talking seriously about clues and possible suspects. No body thought that one day, it would be a fight between a brother and a sister. The family even asked Debra to partake in a polygraph test, but she never did.

If Rachel's mother, Fran Langston, was to be asked, she

believed that Dan James ruined Rusty's view of Debra. As we have already mentioned, Rusty was only 11 years old at the time Rachel, Renee, and Julie went missing, but she could remember very well how he and Debra brainstormed about the possible scenarios. Fran recounted that she collected every newspaper clipping about the disappearance of the girls, and each time, Debra and Rusty would bundle up to negotiate between points. They were closely knitted--until Rusty met Dan James.

Private Investigator Dan James followed the girls' case since 1975. Rusty met him 2 decades later, while Rusty was looking for an investigator who might help him and the others' families uncover the truth of what happened on December 23 of 1974. He was very glad to know that Dan already knew a lot of about the disappearances.

The two developed an instant bond, so much that Dan worked alongside the family even though he was not officially hired. He claimed that he never received any form of compensation for his efforts, and he was okay with it. However, like John Swain, Dan couldn't formally name his resources. All he ever mentioned was how "credible" these sources were. For instance, he said that one witness saw Rachel around Christmas time of 1998. Due to this tip from the "credible witness", Rusty and Dan believed that Rachel had been visiting Fort Worth every

Christmas season.

According to Dan, "someone" was trying to drive the two girls (particularly, Rachel) away from the town, Julie was an unexpected victim, seeing that she was not originally included in the trip. Rusty believed James, and he added that "someone close to the girls had something to do with the disappearance." Due to his dedication to the case, Dan offered $25,000 to whoever would be able to shed some light on the mystery.

He said that his wife would not disagree with his decision to hand out that much money if it would be able to help the girls. He also sponsored the website for the missing trio.

It was also during this time that Debra became a suspect in Rusty's eyes. Debra candidly said that she knew how Rusty believed that she wrote the letter to Thomas. Rusty signed a letter along with Rayanne Mosely, Judy Wilson, and Richard Wilson, which encouraged Debra to perform a polygraph test regarding the case.

Truly, this case had ruined family relations. It placed a crack in the relationship between a sister and a brother, as well as in the bond between a mother and son.

Similarly, Rayanne and her other children experienced difficulties. Back then, Rayanne was not able to tend to her other children because of the disappearance of her daughter, Julie. Her kids, now all grown ups, remembered how they had to fend for themselves. They even went so far as selling cigars and getting married early.

They remembered how atrocious those times were, which is why they value having a solid family now. Rayanne was quoted saying that she believed that her daughter was simply at the wrong place, at the wrong time. She also said that someone out there knew something.

The only family that kept their ground was the Wilsons. It was difficult, they admitted. They came to a point when they hated God. But for their other child, Ricky, they worked hard to move on. For Judy, she chose to believe that the girls were all dead. That was better compared to torture and abuse that they could have suffered if they lived for years after the faithful December 23, 1974.

A recent update about the letter came up saying that the letter had a DNA sample, and it didn't belong to Rachel. Hand writing experts also examined it, and they reported that the letter was written by a right-handed person, while Rachel was a left-handed individual.

The US Postal Service also already determined where it came from: according to them, it didn't come from Eliasville, or from Weatherford, instead it came from within the town of Fort Worth. Up to now, the police still believed that the victims met with a person they knew personally, and afterwards, they were harmed.

Chapter 2: Alyssa Angelique McLemore

Only 21 years old at the time when she disappeared on April 9, 2009, Alyssa Angelique McLemore is now classified as an "Endangered Missing Person". Her disappearance included a sad tale of not being able to be with her sick mother in her last days.

Alyssa lived in Kent, Washington together with her mother and her grandmother. At 6:30 pm, her grandmother talked to her on the phone, urging her to come home because the condition of her mother was becoming worse by the minute. Alyssa's mom had a severe case of an autoimmune disease called scleroderma-- a condition wherein the patient's skin (particularly the connective tissue) hardens and contracts. Before the call ended, Alyssa promised her grandmother to return, so that she would be able to attend to her mother's needs.

She never did.

3 days after Alyssa went missing, her mother died. The family tried everything to reach her, but Alyssa remained missing. A supposed witness said that Alyssa was indeed, in Kent, somewhere near the 30th Avenue South and

Kent-Des Moines Road. The witness also reported that a green pickup truck (1990's model and possibly bore an Oregon license plate), approached her on that day.

While investigating the case, the police found out that a call to 911 was made using Alyssa's phone on April 10, around 9:15 pm. The agent who answered said that she heard a woman's voice asking for help, but since the cellular phone was not equipped with a GPS sensor, they were not able to locate the exact area where the call was made.

After the plea, the line went dead. Despite the obvious lack of info about the call, the dispatcher was still able to determine that the call was from Kent, Washington. Alyssa was probably just close by. A few days after the 911 call, her cellular phone went out of service.

Another clue surfaced when someone confided to the police that before her disappearance, Alyssa was seen to be with a man (who is still unidentified up to now). According to the witness, Alyssa was familiar to the man who was described as a Caucasian, probably in his 50's or 60's, 5'8" in height, and 175-185 pounds in weight. Weird was the fact that, said witness also reported that the man drove a green pickup truck.

For her former boyfriend and father of her then 3-year old

daughter, Albert Walker, Alyssa was not an irresponsible parent. He admitted that sometimes Alyssa would go out for one day, but she would always return the next morning. He also added that, as a doting mother, she would never intentionally abandon their three year old. "It's not like her, not like her at all," Albert said during an interview.

When Tina Russell, Alyssa's aunt was interviewed, she expressed confusion as to how the 911 dispatcher was not able to locate the call. According to her, Alyssa had a new Blackberry phone, which most probably had a GPS. She also added: "...they can do pings off the last two towers to find out where the call came from, so what's taking so long?"

Even Alyssa's friend of 9 years, Melissa Moore, assisted in the search. Considering herself as Alyssa's big sister, she hoped that her friend would return, but when no sign of Alyssa showed up on the day of her mother's funeral, she started to worry deeply. Melissa initiated a candlelight vigil on East Hill and a car-wash fund raising to help finance the search. She said that for Alyssa's daughter, she wouldn't give up hoping that her friend was safe.

By 2012, the police had three binders full of information about Alyssa's case-- there were many leads, but no solid clue as to where she was. They came close with having at least some form of closure when a woman's body was found in Lewis County, but the remains did not belong to Alyssa. Even people who were not personally or officially engaged to the case were trying to look out for possible clues.

For instance, one investigator from King County Medical Examiner's Office admitted that whenever they saw a young woman being brought to the medical examiner, they would immediately compare it to Alyssa's description and clothing.

Since her grandmother, Barbara McLemore, no longer needed a big home, she opted to relocate in Auburn. She tried to make the news of her relocation become as known as possible, just in case Alyssa returned.

6 years after she disappeared, will new clues emerge? That is the big question. The only clues so far were the phone call, the pickup truck which approached her on the day she went missing, and the man she was seen with before she disappeared. The phone could have already been destroyed, considering the fact that it went out of service immediately after 911 was contacted. The pickup truck was very hard to identify without the exact license plate. And the older man she was seen with had very vague descriptions.

It was 6 years ago since Neveah, Alyssa's daughter, lost her mother. If Alyssa never returns, all she would have are stories: that her mother enjoyed dancing, doted on her when she was a baby, and that she was a devoted daughter and grandchild.

The "We Must Find Alyssa McLemore" Facebook page is still present, but visiting it will only give someone the feeling that there's no longer hope. The last post in the page was on 2011, and it wasn't even about Alyssa's case. According to the poster, another teen from Renon was missing, too. And the teen had similarities with Alyssa (who also had Asian descent).

Chapter 3: Joseph Force Crater

Have you ever heard of the word "missingest"? Well, it's not really a term, but when the disappearance of Joseph Crater happened in the year 1930-- he became the "missingest" person in New York.

On January 5, 1889, Joseph Force Crater was born in Pennsylvania USA, even though his parents were both of Irish descent. In 1916, he was able to obtain his law degree from Columbia University. From a simple clerk, he became a successful lawyer who had a lot of political connections all over New York.

At a glance, he would seem like a good lawyer, but many people from his time believed that he was able to obtain his position, which was Associate Justice in the New York State Supreme Court, through his shady participation with organized crime, or his connection to the Tammany Hall Democratic Organization. According to rumors, Joseph "paid" for his new position.

Well, people became suspicious primarily because of the way he handled financial dealings. The most controversial, perhaps, was when he withdrew $20,000 around the time he became appointed as interim justice. That money was almost equal to his yearly salary, and was the typical wage for an employee at the Tammany Hall. What did he do with the money? Well, he purchased a bankrupted hotel building.

He did nothing with the building though-- he didn't revive it, nor did he open up a new business. In fact, he sold it later in the year for $75,000 to a mortgage firm. New York City later on bought the said building, but the price was a whopping $3,000,000. But when the building got in the way of a road widening project, it was instantly demolished.

His personal life also reflected his shady character in politics and justice. Joseph was a married man since 1917, to a woman named Stella Mance Wheeler, who was also his previous client. Reports said that Joseph kept his girlfriends on the sides, but he was still a "devoted" husband. In June 1930, when the court was in recess, they moved to their Belgrade Lakes summer house in Maine.

A month after that, Joseph received a phone call and then told his wife that he had to head out to New York to straighten a couple of things out. He assured Stella that it was nothing serious. Apparently, it was really nothing serious because on August 1, he returned to Maine, but not without visiting one of his girlfriends in Atlantic City, New Jersey.

However, his stay in Maine didn't last long. On August 3, he set out to return to New York, yet again. He promised Stella that he would return in a couple of days, especially on her birthday which was on August 9. In fact, Joseph already bought a canoe as a gift to his wife. Stella agreed, of course, especially since she noticed that Joseph was in a good mood while he packed.

Back in New York, nothing was amiss with Joseph. He stayed in their apartment at 5th avenue and he went to his office to work. On August 6, his assistant reported that Joseph stayed in the office for 2 hours-- he simply removed locked files from several briefcases and brought them home. He said that Joseph also destroyed some files. On that day, his assistant remembered him cashing out checks worth $5,000 before telling him he could go.

It was also on August 6, 1930, when Joseph got a ticket to watch *Dancing Partner*, a Broadway performance to be held at the Belasco Theater. Before heading out to watch the performance, Joseph met with his friend and fellow lawyer, William Klein, and one of his girlfriends, a showgirl named Sally Ritz.

The three met at *Billy Haas's Chophouse*, which was in Manhattan, particularly in 300 block of West 45th street. At around 9:15 pm, Joseph left his companions behind, probably to watch the performance at Belasco Theater.

William and Sally remembered he hailed a cab, which was tan-colored.

He was never seen again. When news of this disappearance spread, taxi services were investigated, but no cab reported picking him up.

Her birthday way passed, Stella became absolutely worried when on August 16 (10 days since her husband was last seen), Joseph was still nowhere in sight. She sent someone to look for him, but the chauffeur returned empty handed. He said that their apartment looked okay. Stella decided to return to New York and see for herself.

The chauffeur was right-- the apartment was organized. All of Joseph's clothes were still in the closet and his monogrammed watch, card case, and pen, which were his most priced possessions, were all safe.

Stella reported Joseph as missing, but the police delayed doing an investigation right away because they believed that Joseph would return soon. When August 25 came and Joseph was still absent- the police thought that something more serious had happened, so they began the investigation. It was because August 25 was the opening of court sessions and Joseph was supposed to attend it.

Months went by and all the evidence about Joseph's case were substantial, but they still could not decide whether the lawyer was dead or alive somewhere. On January of 1931, Stella returned home to their apartment in 5th Avenue and found a chest drawer with 4 envelopes. One envelope contained more than $6,000 cash, checks worth $2,600 all signed and payable to Joseph Force Crater, and three other checks which were worth a little more than $500.

The second envelope was Joseph's will which named Stella as the beneficiary of everything he owned. The third envelope contained the details of Joseph's life insurance-- the amount was $30,000, and the beneficiary was again, his wife. The last envelope contained a list of the people who owned Joseph some money. It was signed "*Love, Joe. This is all confidential.*"

There was also childish scribble which could be read as "*Am very weary.*" OR "*I'm very sorry.*" According to the Jury, the letters could have been written before September 1, so it was possible that someone broke into the apartment. The police also said that they searched the apartment 5 months prior, and they didn't find the envelopes.

Could it be Stella? According to reports, she already had the papers for a few days before she surrendered it to the authorities. She also said that the police might have just missed the drawer because it was not located in plain sight.

Her opinion was that Joseph wrote the list of debts under duress, possibly after he disappeared on August 6, and then someone broke into the apartment and placed the envelopes where she could see it. The police, however, insisted that the apartment was under surveillance since September 4 of 1930. They only stopped monitoring it after Stella returned home in January of the next year. Speculations rose that Stella had seen the letters way before January, but she stood her ground that she had seen it only in that month.

Because she believed so much that her husband was a victim of foul play, she sued several insurance companies even after 7 years of the case. The insurance companies, of course, won the lawsuits especially since solid evidence was lacking. By 1939, at her request, Joseph Crater was declared legally dead. Stella would soon remarry, and it would end up in divorce. In 1961, her book entitled *The Empty Robe* was published. It was about her life and Joseph's disappearance.

75 years after the fact, the police collected a new lead. When Stella Ferrucci-Good died in April of 2005, her belongings included an enveloped marked with "Do Not Open Until My Death". Inside the envelope was a letter which talked about three men who murdered Joseph.

According to Stella, the perpetrators were her own husband (who worked as a Parks Department Supervisor and a life guard), a police officer who worked in New York, and the officer's brother who was a cab driver. The letter also specified the burial site, which was in Coney Island in Brooklyn, particularly near Eight Street.

The burial site stated in the letter was already the foundation of *New York Aquarium* now. During its establishment, skeletal remains from 5 people were found but they are now in Potter's field along with thousands of other remains. On top of this difficulty, it would be hard to have Joseph's DNA, as he didn't have a close relative-- the closest he would have now are the grandchildren of his brother. Dental records are also out of the question since he wore dentures.

Whether Stella Ferrucci-Good's letter was telling the truth or not, we may never find out.

Chapter 4: Brooke Henson

The case of twenty-year-old Brooke Henson—known to her friends and family as Brookey—is a bit of a double-whammy: not only does this case contain a mysterious disappearance with no leads, but it also involves a matter of stolen identity.

Brooke was last seen on July 4, 1999, when her parents, Martin and Cathy, came home from a concert in Charlotte, NC, to find their daughter sitting on the porch of their South Carolinian home at two in the morning while a party went on inside. Brooke had fought with her boyfriend, Shaun Shirley, earlier in the evening, she told them, and appeared very emotional.

When Brooke, in tears, told her father she planned on breaking up with her boyfriend and leaving town—even commenting she'd "be back in five years"—Martin Henson was not upset. Not only had his daughter run away before; she'd also broken up with her boyfriend (a well-known and feared local criminal) several times. Brooke then informed them she was about to leave to buy cigarettes at a nearby store—the only one in their small, charming town of Travelers Rest.

Departing on foot, Brooke left behind a note for her boyfriend to come after her if he cared. She left around 2:30 a.m. While the store was only two blocks from her home, Brooke did not return; she has never been seen nor heard from since.

Caucasian with blonde hair (which was dyed brown at the time of her disappearance), brown eyes, pierced ears, and a penchant for Marlboro cigarettes, Brooke was last seen in a tan sleeveless shirt, deep green shorts, black sandals, and a watch on her left arm, as well as a bracelet on the right—both of which were silver.

Shaun Shirley, Brooke's boyfriend and ten years her senior, had a criminal record of sexual assault and drug charges. Despite his argument that night with Brooke, his record, and his refusal to help with the investigation of his girlfriend's whereabouts, Shirley had never been publicly named a suspect possibly because of the lack of evidence to actually link him with the disappearance.

According to family members, police waited three weeks after Brooke went missing to begin their search efforts, believing she left on her own, possibly as a result of her boyfriend's treatment. When interviews with friends and family revealed it would be out-of-character for Brooke to leave without warning anyone, police began to suspect abduction—or even murder.

In 2006, it appeared Brooke's whereabouts were no longer a mystery. Someone called the police department and told them that he knew where Brooke Henson was. According to the caller, Brooke was an honor student in Columbia University and Ivy League. The caller was later revealed to be a Manhattan employer that informed authorities that a woman named Brooke Henson had just applied for a nanny and housekeeper position.

When the employer ran a background check (only through Google), Henson's name came up as a missing person, arousing their suspicions.

As police probed further, however, it became clear this Brooke Henson was a fraud; she was actually a woman by the name of Esther Reed, who'd simply stolen Henson's identity to obtain her GED (Reed, like Henson, was a high school dropout). As Brooke, Reed attended Columbia University—studying, rather ironically, criminology and psychology—and accumulated over $100,000 of student loan debt in Henson's name.

Reed was a seasoned identity thief, having already pulled this scam under several false names and social security numbers before. Since her mother's death in 1999, the Montana-native had been attending other universities such as Harvard, obtaining passports, and crafting elaborate life stories for herself, fooling new friends, professors, employers, and boyfriends.

When police approached her in the university dorms, Reed claimed she actually was Brooke. Citing domestic abuse and using details from Brooke's life (obtained from the internet articles surrounding Brooke's case), Reed tried to assure police she'd left home of her own will, and just wanted to get on with her new life and continue her academic pursuits.

She even agreed to take a DNA test to confirm her identity. When the test date came along, however, Reed was a no-show; she went on the run, taking only her cat and a few toiletries...yet leaving behind an indisputable trail of evidence against herself.

In 2008, a year and a half after her stint as Brooke Henson, Reed was arrested in Chicago, IL. In court and interviews, she claimed she did not mean to cause anyone pain with her thefts, and only wished to escape her rough past and strained family ties. Her lawyer told the jury Reed made poor decisions due to mental illness, caused by childhood abuse and trauma.

While Reed was the youngest of eight and had very strict religious parents, her siblings did not confirm her claims of abuse. Reed claimed her student loans were intended to be paid back—unlike all the debts under her other identities—because she had planned to live as Brooke Henson for the rest of her life, truly believing she would never be caught. In fact, Reed got away with her new identity for over two years, without ever raising suspicion.

Reed received a four-year prison sentence for her identity theft and fraud crimes, to be served in West Virginia. Despite her record, Reed is not believed to be involved in Henson's disappearance; it's believed she simply stumbled upon Brooke's story while searching for a new identity to steal.

Today, officials continue to investigate Brooke's disappearance as a murder case. Although one suspect exists, a lack of evidence prevents conviction. Every year on July 4th, the anniversary of the last day Brook was seen, the Henson family has a candlelight vigil at the local police station to remind officials of how poorly they handled her case, failing to treat it as a homicide sooner and follow proper protocol. Out of all Travelers Rest's Missing Persons cases, Brooke Henson's is the only one to remain unsolved.

Unfortunately, Cathy and Martin Henson did not remain married, presumably due to the extreme stress and grief following Brooke's disappearance. Ill with severe anxiety and multiple sclerosis, respectively, the Hensons clung to hope that their daughter was still alive for several years—five, in fact, the same seemingly sarcastic number their daughter gave them the night of her disappearance—but now appear to side with police that the evidence, little as there is, points to homicide.

As for leads in the case, none currently exist; Brooke's former boyfriend, rumored to have invited Henson to leave Shaun Shirley and run away with him, died of a drug overdose in an apparent suicide before officials could question him. It's presently believed Brooke was murdered near River Falls, a popular party spot for Travelers Rest youth, although all tips have hit dead ends.

The whereabouts of Brooke Henson are still unknown, more than fifteen years later. A $7,000 reward has since been posted, with neighbors, family, friends, and anonymous donors contributing to the fund, in the hopes someone will provide clues to Brooke's case.

The Travelers Rest, SC and Police urge anyone with information regarding Brooke to come forward—and, perhaps, bring her loved ones some closure to their drawn-out nightmare.

Chapter 5: Maura Murray

On February 5, 2004, twenty-one-year-old Maura Murray received a distressing phone call at her job monitoring security for the University of Massachusetts-Amherst, where she was also a student. Before she hung up, Maura began to cry and was so upset, a superior had to walk her home.

Despite the scene, Maura seemed fine a couple of days later, when her father, Fred Murray, took her out for dinner and used-car shopping. Afterwards, Fred returned to his hotel, letting his daughter borrow his car.

That night, Maura crashed Fred's car and apologized to him profusely. He and his daughter decided to meet Monday night to discuss insurance options and file the proper claims.

On February 9, the night Maura was due to meet her father, the nursing student drove out of Massachusetts after telling professors there had been a death in her family (which was later found to be false) and packed her car for an unknown trip.

In New Hampshire, Maura's car lost traction and spun off Route 112 in North Haverhill around 7:30 in the evening. While the windshield was broken and air bags deployed,

Maura was not found in or near her vehicle—which police say was locked and smelled strongly of alcohol, specifically wine, a box of which was in the backseat.

A witness, Butch Atwood, told police he'd asked if Maura needed the police. She said no, but Atwood called anyway. By the time police arrived, Maura had vanished. Her phone and credit cards were not in the car, although everything she'd packed remained inside.

Some investigators believe Maura left to start a new life and escape past run-ins with the law (one theory is that she fled to Canada), or that the mysterious call she'd received four days prior had something to do with her decision to pick up and leave so quickly. Perhaps, some investigators speculate, she'd crashed on purpose. Another theory is that Maura was suicidal, staging an abduction to avoid hurting her loved ones, but friends and family are skeptical, especially her father.

Fred Murray didn't believe his daughter would ever leave, at least not without informing him at some point, and does not believe she'd commit suicide. Today, over a decade later, Fred maintains that his daughter was abducted after her crash and murdered—the only explanation, he feels, for why she wouldn't call him and let him know she's alright.

While the leads in Maura's case were promising at first, they led police nowhere: phone records, detailing Maura's inquiries to nearby hotels and a lodge her family frequented; directions to a town in Vermont; the direction of the car before it spun off the road. Lieutenant John Healy, though retired, continues to investigate Maura's case, despite the fact the leads—numerous as they are— have provided no clear answers.

It's a strange case, to say the least. No one knows what, exactly, the phone call Maura received on the 5th was about, or who was on the end of that line. All possible sightings and whereabouts have hit dead ends, from a voicemail on her boyfriend's cell phone—the sound of a young woman sobbing, thirty-six hours after the crash—to a sighting in Hillsboro, NH, involving another young woman fitting Maura's description, mouthing, "Help me" to a store clerk while an older man accompanied her. Neither tip could be confirmed or traced.

Stranger still, the Murrays did not display behavior typical for families in similar circumstances: Fred Murray, for all his insistence that Maura was abducted, allegedly faked his search efforts for the first year after his daughter's disappearance. Two search volunteers and another daughter's ex-husband claimed Fred would sleep late, exercise and eat breakfast, then briefly search for Maura before returning to the bar of his hotel.

In the presence of police and journalists, Fred showed high emotions and a sense of urgency...both of which apparently disappeared as soon as investigators and news teams left.

Additionally—also very unlike families of missing persons—the Murrays never organized a website or online search. Maura's official search website is run by a family friend who calls herself an aunt, yet is not actually related to Maura. Maura's siblings and mother did very little apparently, to aid in the search efforts.

Fred told many of his daughter's friends to avoid talking to reporters—an extremely suspicious move, as was Fred's refusal to cooperate with state detectives for two years after Maura disappeared. When he finally agreed to speak with them, he brought a team of two lawyers and sued the department under the belief they were withholding information from him. It was also discovered that Fred lied to investigators about certain details of the night he took Maura to dinner.

James Renner, an author who had been investigating Maura's case, said there were several odd facts about the Murray family that bring even more suspicion to the disappearance. An old and decrepit house where Fred used to reside contained adult magazines with Fred Murray's name on them; inside were copies of photographs of Fred's young female cousins.

Maura, just a few weeks before her crash, had stolen someone else's identity and credit card information—and prior to that, while attending West Point, she'd stolen from Fort Knox. After transferring to the University of Massachusetts, Maura began an affair with a track coach. The two were reported to have discussed running away together.

In 2010, Kurt Murray wrote a song for his missing sister. The lyrics describe his belief that Maura disappeared on purpose, in search of a new life post-tragedy, although no one has admitted to knowing what, exactly, that tragedy might entail.

What began as a seemingly straightforward case—girl crashes car and gets abducted—quickly turned into a deeper mystery than officials first imagined, and has only become more mysterious as the years pass. Most investigators and followers of the Murray case believe Maura, who had military training and could survive in the wild if she had to, as well as a brother-in-law with CIA ties, left of her own accord—and that her family knows exactly where she is.

The Murrays' strange actions strongly suggested involvement from all family members in Maura's "disappearance." With the right connections and support, it is entirely possible for a person to simply drop his or her old life and begin anew, without a single lead as to where they went.

On the other hand, investigators know an absence of proof is not proof of absence; the fact that there was not any proof of foul play in Maura's case does not mean there was no foul play. It is possible that she was abducted or even murdered, and officials will continue to investigate her case according to the proper protocol.

Most are highly suspect, however, of Maura's actions prior to her accident: the strange timeline of events that took place on February 9, and the bizarre behavior of her family members following her disappearance—particularly those of her father, Fred.

Chapter 6: The Beaumont Children

The disappearance of a child is always treated with urgent priority, and the disappearance of all three Beaumont children—nine-year-old Jane, seven-year-old Arnna, and four-year-old Grant—was no exception.

On January 26, 1966, Jane Beaumont, extremely responsible for her age and very shy, led her younger siblings to Glenelg Beach to play and join in the celebrations of Australia Day in the suburb of Somerton Park, Adelaide, Australia. At ten in the morning, the children took the bus to the beach, only five minutes away, and were told to return home by noon. Their father, Jim, was meeting clients in Snowtown, while their mother, Nancy, visited a friend for the morning.

Nancy got home just before noon, but her children weren't on board the scheduled bus. Because the children sometimes walked home, Nancy thought they might arrive a little later, or perhaps they would catch the two o'clock bus.

Two more buses arrived, and Jim returned home from work; the Beaumont children had still not arrived. It was so unlike responsible Jane, who took rules seriously. The distressed Beaumont parents decided to search Glenelg Beach themselves. When they could not find the children, nor any of their belongings, they reported them missing at 7:30 in the evening, and Jim continued his search throughout the night.

While the case is old—today, the children would be in their fifties—it's by no means closed; despite several confirmed sightings of the children that day, as well as many suspects, the Beaumont children were never found.

The bus driver and a woman on board confirmed that the children boarded at 10:10 in the morning, and got off at the Moseley Street stop near the beach five minutes later. The woman was able to confirm what clothes the children wore, and noted Jane was carrying the book *Little Women*.

Nearly an hour later, Somerton Park's postal worker saw the children heading towards the beach—although he changed his timeframe when recollecting the sighting to police.

An elderly woman sitting outside a sailing club noticed the Beaumont children playing in a sprinkler at the Colley Reserve at eleven a.m. Nearby on the grass—appearing to watch as the children played—was a blond man in a blue swimsuit, who began to play with the kids a few minutes later.

The next sighting, at Wenzel's Cake Shop, took place just fifteen minutes before noon, when the children were due home. In addition to their usual purchase of treats, the kids ordered a meat-pie. It was not something they typically got, according to the shopkeeper. They paid with a one-pound note, despite the fact Nancy Beaumont had given Jane nothing but shillings and sixpence coins. It's possible the man in blue trunks gave the children the extra money, although police have never been able to confirm this.

At noon, it was reported by a woman, an elderly couple, and their granddaughter that they'd seen a man matching the description of the blond man from the lawn—and that three children, matching the description of the Beaumont children, were with him. He asked if they'd seen someone touching his clothes nearby, perhaps stealing his money.

They said no, and the man returned to the kids and proceeded to get them dressed. This struck the witnesses as strange, since at least one of the kids appeared more than old enough to dress herself.

Approximately fifteen minutes later, the man and the children, according to a witness, walked behind the beach hotel and seemed to go into the changing rooms near the area where the Beaumonts had been spotted playing in the sprinkler. This account seemed to be the final sighting of the missing kids that police could confirm.

Two more sightings, unable to be verified, were reported that day: about fifteen minutes before two p.m., a witness saw a man and three children leaving the beach, although he said the man had light brown hair, not blond. Additionally, the postman's account was investigated. He said the Beaumont kids were by themselves, and could not remember if he'd seen them just before two, p.m., or just before three.

Search efforts for the Beaumont children were among the largest in Australian history. While some initially believed the children drowned, the lack of any belongings—towels, clothes, or Jane's book—left behind on the beach, coupled with multiple sightings of the kids with the man in the blue swimsuit, point almost squarely at abduction.

While the suspect is unknown, it's likely the children knew him personally (as it was unlikely they'd go willingly with a complete stranger) or that he convinced them he knew their parents. One investigative journalist theorizes that the meat-pie the children purchased was later drugged by the man, to make the children appear at ease and less shy than usual.

On January 31, 1966, five days after his children went missing, Jim Beaumont appeared on television and pleaded for his kids' safe return on a national broadcast. Immediately, hundreds of tips flooded in—and, though police took every lead seriously, none of the tips led to new information.

Psychic and parapsychological investigations were initiated after the Beaumonts' disappearance, but neither yielded results. All possible suspects, including known kidnappers and murderers, were cleared of any connection to the children upon further investigation, except for one: Bevan Spencer von Einem.

Von Einem confessed to murdering and performing "experimental surgeries" on abducted victims in the area of Adelaide in the 1970s and '80s. While von Einem confessed he'd abducted three children from a beach, and said that he'd often visited Glenelg, it was not confirmed if those children—who von Einem claimed he surgically "connected" before killing them—were the Beaumonts, or if his story was even true.

Unable to convict him for most of his "confessions," officials were finally able to arrest von Einem for the murder of a fifteen-year-old boy. His sentence was life without parole for twenty-four (and later, thirty-six) years.

While it wasn't able to be confirmed, a sighting of von Einem prior to his arrest would place him at Glenelg Beach on January 27, 1966, when divers were searching for the Beaumont children in a drain nearby. Psychologically speaking, this evidence—though circumstantial—is significant because criminals often return to their crime scenes, especially during search efforts.

In addition to a lack of concrete evidence, one flaw with the theory that von Einem abducted the children is that he would have only been twenty—at least ten years younger than the man in the blue swimsuit, according to witnesses.

South Australian officials continue their search for Jane, Arnna, and Grant today, with a posted reward of one million dollars.

Jim and Nancy remained in their home at Somerton Park for several years before filing for divorce and moving elsewhere. They hoped and prayed for over twenty years that their children would return—one reason they did not want to move, despite the heartache and difficult memories their home now held.

Chapter 7: The Missing Marys

Katherine Mary Lyon, aged 10, and her sister, Sheila Mary, aged 12, became the center of one of the most high-profile investigations in Washington D.C. when they mysteriously disappeared during a visit to a shopping mall in Maryland in 1975.

What happened to them and what became of the investigation? Let's find out.

Nothing out of the ordinary

The two girls were born in Kensington, Maryland to Mary and John Lyon. While not living the celebrity life, John was still a known personality since he was a radio disc jockey in WMAL, a local station then managed by the owner of *ABC Television* affiliate in Washington, who was also the owner of the defunct *Washington Star*. Aside from Katherine and Sheila, John and Mary also had another child, an older son whom they named Jay.

The day the girls went missing was just an ordinary day. No one was expecting that a painful mystery would break the hearts of the Lyon Family.

It was March 25, 1975; the kids were on their spring break

so it was only normal for them to stroll around especially since Easter was coming and the community was becoming colorful. On that Tuesday morning, Katherine and Sheila asked their parents to let them go watch the Easter Exhibits in *Wheaton Plaza*, a renowned shopping center half a mile away from their home.

Mary and John agreed on the condition that they should be home by 4:00 in the afternoon. Happy that they got what they wanted, the girls took the $4 from their parents and informed them that they would have lunch at the *Orange Bowl*.

Then, off the girls went; the time was between 11:00 am and 12:00 pm-- it was the last time their parents saw them.

The Timeline

When 7:00 PM came and the girls were still not home, John and Mary decided to enlist the help of the police, who, after a series of investigations, came up with the timeline.

They believed that the girls left home at 11:00 AM; by 1:00 in the afternoon, they were outside the *Orange Bowl*, as reported by a child from the neighborhood who also told the police that the sisters were talking to an unidentified man. At 2:00 PM, Jay, their older brother, saw them eating pizza together inside the *Orange Bowl*. By 2:30 PM to 3:00 in the afternoon, a friend saw them together walking down the street which, according to reports, was "one of the most direct routes from the mall to their home".

After that, no one saw Katherine and Sheila again.

The unidentified man seen talking to the girls was described by the child witness as someone who was 50-60 years old; he was wearing a brown suit, was carrying a suitcase, and was about 6 feet tall. Additionally, the young witness mentioned that the briefcase contained a tape recorder and a microphone. Other kids who also talked to the man were also said to have spoken to the microphone for unknown reasons.

This led the police to believe that he should be considered as the primary suspect, hence two composite sketches were released and scattered in the hope that someone would be able to pinpoint the man's identity and whereabouts.

Unacknowledged Links

After the sketches were released several people came forward and reported that the man was also seen in several shopping malls in the nearby Prince George County, Maryland. Two of the malls he allegedly visited were: *Marlow Heights Shopping Center* and the *Iverson Mall*. On those occasions, he was witnessed talking to young girls, asking them to read an answering machine script written in the index card to the microphone he carried.

Despite the similarity in the scenarios present in *Wheaton Plaza*, the authorities were unable to make a solid connection between the reports.

Not Much Hope

As the weeks wore on, the family and the police became more agitated-- they knew that the longer the case remained cold, the slimmer the chances were of finding the girls. Multiple volunteer groups carried out searches on vacant lots and stream beds, yet still, not one clue was recovered. On May 23, 1975, Maryland Lt. Governor Blair Lee, ordered 122 National Guardsmen to participate in a search operation to be performed at the Montgomery County forest. However, no matter how extensive the search operations were, Katherine and Sheila remained missing.

False Leads

Perhaps one of the hardest parts of searching for your missing loved ones was receiving a valuable lead and then finding out later on that they were not connected to the case. This happened to the Lyon family a couple of times, and each was more heartbreaking than the last.

A set of false leads were sent through phone calls to the Lyon family's home, claiming that they had the girls and they wanted money in exchange for their safe return. One of the most seemingly-credible calls was placed by a man on April 4; he asked John Lyon to fill a briefcase with $10,000 cash and then leave it at the restroom of Annapolis, Maryland courthouse.

John followed the instructions, but the briefcase was never claimed. Later, the same man called again, telling the Lyon family that he couldn't retrieve the money because the courthouse was filled with policemen. As a response, he was told that for him to peacefully receive the ransom money, he would need to show some evidence that the sisters were truly in his custody. The man said he would contact the family again, but he never did.

On April 7, about two weeks after the disappearance, a witness came forward and offered a valuable account: two girls who seemed to look like Sheila and Katherine were seen at the rear side of a beige 1968 Ford station wagon at Manassas, Virginia-- they were gagged and bound.

The witness said that when the driver, who also looked like the man in the released composite sketch, noticed that someone was tailing him, he "ran a red light" and sped to Route 234, going to Interstate 66, Virginia.

Thinking smart, the witness looked closely at the plate number of the vehicle and was able to identify it as a Maryland License; the combination was DMT-6**, where in the last two digits were unknown because the plate was bent. Several people who were armed with CB (citizen band) radios roamed the areas in the hope that they would spot the beige 1968 Ford station wagon, but the operation was unsuccessful.

Despite the "media firestorm" brought about by the witnesses' reports, police still claimed it to be "questionable", although they didn't offer any more explanation as to why.

The Suspects

Throughout the investigation, several names came up as the suspects to the Lyon Sisters' disappearance; one of them was Raymond Rudolf Mileski Sr. who, in 1977, murdered his wife and son after a sordid family dispute. It was reported that Raymond moved to Suitland, Maryland in 1975-- Suitland was near Prince George County where the man with the microphone was seen roaming some shopping centers.

From informant tips and Raymond's own claims that he knew something about the Lyon Sisters, law authorities treated him as a suspect; however, in 1982, the police searched his home but found no evidence that could link him to the case. Raymond was convicted due to the homicide of his family-- he was supposed to spend 40 years in prison, but he died in 2004 while serving time.

Fred Howard Coffey was another suspect although not once did he claim that he knew anything about Katherine and Sheila. What the police were certain of was that he was employed at Silver Spring, Maryland, 6 days after the girls' disappearance-- Silver Spring was near *Wheaton Plaza*. On top of that, he was also a violent man who was incarcerated in 1987 due to the 1979 slaying of a 10 year old girl in North Carolina. Still, despite a thorough investigation, no links could be produced between him and the Lyon Sisters.

It Could Be Him

In the middle of the ruckus, the investigation, and the

search operations, one friend of the family reported to the police that aside from the unidentified man with the briefcase, another young man acted suspiciously on the day of the disappearance.

This young man was said to be staring so intently at the girls in a 'creepy' fashion that the witness confronted him about it. Reportedly, the strange guy was a Caucasian, with long hair, acne on the face, and scars on his left cheek. A composite sketch was released and surprisingly, it looked like the mugshot photo of Lloyd Welch.

The interesting bit was, Lloyd Welch acted as if he was a witness rather than a suspect.

Apparently, on the day the article about the man with the microphone was released, Lloyd came back to *Wheaton Plaza*, approached a security guard, and reported that he had been there on the day the girls went missing. Lloyd added that after the brown-suited man talked to the girls, he later forced them inside his car in an act of abduction.

Alarmed by this, the security guard called the police and Lloyd Welch was brought to the station where he was interviewed and subjected to a polygraph test; in the end he conceded that he provided false information about the kidnapping. He was then promptly released by the authorities.

Lloyd's innocence stayed for so long until December of 2014, when his cousin, Henry Parker, admitted to the police that in the year 1975, he helped Lloyd dump two heavy duffel bags into a fire. According to Henry's statement, they met at a property at Taylor's Mountain Road in Thaxton, Virginia, where he saw Lloyd carrying two army style duffel bags, each weighing around 60 to 70 pounds and smelt like "death". Without asking about the bags' contents, Henry threw them onto the fire after his cousin transferred them into his hold.

At this point, Lloyd was already in prison, serving time for a child molestation case. On July of 2015, he was indicted for his alleged involvement in the disappearance and murder of Katherine and Sheila Lyon.

As of this moment, Lloyd Welch, now 58, is in Bedford County awaiting trial. If ever he stood trial for the sisters' abduction and presumed death, then it's going to be a bodiless murder case as the remains of the sisters are still yet to be found.

After the girls' vanishing, John worked as a victim counselor while Jay became a policeman, probably as a tribute to the sisters who haven't got the justice they deserved.

Chapter 8: Asha's Pre-Dawn Adventures

Asha Degree's disappearance case boggled the minds of many, and now, it's about to disturb yours. On Valentine's Day of the year 2000, 9 year old Asha appeared to have left home, alone, and with no one knowing what was on her mind. Whether she had prior plans that she wanted to be kept secret, or she was smoothly abducted, is still any one's guess up to this day.

14th of February, Year 2000

Asha lived with her parents and brother at Oak Street in Shelby, North Carolina. On the early morning of February 14, at around 6:30, their mother went to their room only to find Asha gone; her brother said he heard "noises" in the early morning hours, but he thought that it was only Asha shuffling around. Furthermore, the girl's father asserted that before he went to sleep, he checked on the two kids at 2:30 am, and they were both there.

Immediately after realizing that their daughter was missing, the distraught parents called the police and an investigation started right away.

They learned from two truck drivers that Asha was

walking on north of Shelby at Highway 18 at around 3:30 am and 4:15 am. After that, she was seen running off to the woods, then the trace ran cold; the highway where she was last seen was just a mile away from their home.

Abduction or Adventure?

The law authorities believed that Asha left on her own accord-- she wasn't abducted. The question was, why did she leave? From reports, it was apparent that Asha was a shy, but happy girl. Her home life was peaceful, and so was her life at school. So it was a real wonder why she left...

Her parents said that a day before she went missing, Asha became visibly upset because their basketball team lost a game; however, she did calm down after a few hours. So it couldn't possibly be the reason behind her vanishing...

The next angle was about the book that Asha's class had read: *The Whipping Boy* by Sid Fleischman. The story was about a prince and a boy who received lashes at the royal palace; the two boys ran away and their adventure became the essence of the book. At the end of the story, both boys returned home safely-- sadly, Asha didn't have the same fate. It also wasn't clear if the story had anything to do with her disappearance.

In an act of preparation?

What further sealed the police's theory that Asha left home at her own volition, was the absence of several personal items in her room, like: a white, long-sleeve t-shirt with a purple lettering, blue jeans with red stripes, a red vest with black trim, black sneakers, long sleeve-black and white shirt, black overalls with *Tweety Bird* design, and a *Tweety Bird* purse.

The black book bag where Asha often kept the house keys was also missing. The parents also reported that all the doors were locked the morning they found her gone. It was as if Asha had prepared for her departure and she had locked the door after stepping out.

On February 17, 3 days after she disappeared, some of Asha's items (marker, *Mickey Mouse* hair bow, and pencil) were discovered at the doorway of a tool shed at *Turner's Upholstery*, which was located at Highway 18. The police did an extensive search in the area, but it yielded nothing significant.

Bitter Progress

18 months after Asha went missing, on August of 2001, a

contractor found her book bag, complete with her name on it, off Highway 18. The depressing part was, it was "double-wrapped" using a black trash bag and was buried-- an indication that someone was intent on hiding it (or preserving it?). Even more disturbing was the fact that the bag was recovered 26 miles away from Asha's home, and it was in a different direction from where she was seen walking.

Clearly thinking that the book bag was evidence, the police immediately sent it to the laboratory for analysis, and although they didn't release the results, it was apparent that they found something significant for after that, they announced that the disappearance was now a criminal matter and foul play could have been involved.

Questions

Asha's case was not as open as others were; through the years, people who loved mysteries had (and still have) pointed out some strange bits in the disappearance.

First and foremost, the reason why Asha "left" was extravagantly unclear. From anyone's point of view, it was evident why the police thought that she left on her own accord, after all, it seemed like she had prepared for it; still not much explanation was given except for the basketball game they had lost and the book they had read.

Unlike other cases, her parents were not mentioned much and no accounts from Asha's friends were included. The reports said that she was pretty much a happy child-- shy but well-adjusted. Which ultimately brings back the question: why did she see the need to leave?

Did something make her curious? Was she meeting someone? Surely, a 9 year old was not so smart as not to have left clues for her parents or her friends. She must have mentioned something to someone if she planned on going away.

Next was the issue with her parents. In most cases, the closest to the victim was the first to be suspected, but in Asha's case, her parents were not reported to have been investigated-- it was as if the police took their explanation and accepted it right away. Some mystery enthusiasts found it weird that her father in particular was not examined, especially since he was the last one who saw Asha before she "left".

Some of the reports even hinted that there was more to this case than meets the eye. The director of National Center for Missing and Exploited Children, Ben Ermini even said that "Kids usually don't start running away until the age of 12." And the director of N.C. Center for Missing

Persons, John Goad even added: "I don't think a case like hers has ever happened anywhere, anytime."

Come to think of it: if Asha went away voluntarily, then why didn't she take anything that could protect her from the cold weather? Her mother even said that she didn't pack any hat, coat or mittens.

Contradicting: that was what Asha's parents' views on the matter were, or at least, they appeared to be. Her mother said that she fully believed that her daughter left wilfully, but her father stated that he couldn't wrap his mind around the idea that she would go somewhere alone, especially since she was scared of dogs.

All in all, the consensus was unanimous: the case lacked significant amounts of information like:

1. Did Asha prepare in the sense that she combed her hair, brushed her teeth, took a bath or got dressed properly? Aside from packing, a girl who was set on leaving would have done at least one of these things. For now, we only know that she didn't do the last one for her mother stated that no coat was missing from her wardrobe-- hence, she was not dressed properly.

2. Did her father truly see her in her room at 2:30 AM? If so, it meant that Asha prepared very fast for her to be seen by the truck driver at around 3:30 AM. A normal

person can walk 1 mile in 20 minutes, but remember that she was 9 years old and was strolling down the road in cold weather.

3. What did the police find out in the lab results of the book bag? Were there fingerprints? Why would someone bury it off Highway 18, and why would that someone wrap it twice using a trash bag and bury it?

4. What was the connection of the tool shed to the case? Why were some of her things found there? Was it always accessible to kids like Asha? Could she have possibly used the place as a rendezvous point before?

5. A child who was afraid of dogs and the dark couldn't possibly have decided to run to the woods off the highway; why would Asha do that? Was she running away from something?

To date, Asha's case is still unsolved.

Chapter 9: Night of Fun

Living Simple

Lauren Spierer was a native of Greenburgh, New York, a town in Westchester County. Her parents, Charlene and Robert (an accountant) supported her studies and curricular activities in Edgemont High School in Greenville. After she graduated in 2009, she took up textile merchandising at Indiana University.

At IU, Lauren became an active member of the Jewish community; in fact, during some of her spring breaks, she would be sent to Israel to plant trees on behalf of the Jewish National Fund.

Her social life was also exciting: she was a part of a regular summer gathering in Camp Towanda and it is here where she would meet her future boyfriend, Jesse Wolff and future IU friends like Jay Rosenbaum.

All in all, it was obvious that Lauren had a life ahead of her. Only, it would be cut short.

Toxic

On June 3, 2011, Lauren decided to be a teenager and have some fun by going to a party at a local bar. Her boyfriend, Jesse, decided to skip the gathering, but he still texted Lauren numerous times before he hit the sack. He never thought that he was texting an inebriated Lauren, and he didn't realize that it would be their last text exchange.

Using the CCTV footage and witnesses' accounts, the police were able to release a timeline of her activities before she went missing. Let's follow her trail.

A half hour past midnight, Lauren was reported to have left her apartment with a friend named David Rohn; together, they went to Jay Rosenbaum's place where Jay's neighbor, Cory Rossman also joined them later.

At 1:46 AM, Lauren was seen entering *Kilroy's Sports Bar*. What she did there was anyone's guess, but a lot of accounts mentioned that she was drinking heavily. At 2:27 AM, Lauren and Cory Rossman were seen exiting the bar; she was barefoot because she left her shoes at *Kilroy's*, and worse, she also left her phone.

At 2:30 AM, it seemed like Cory did what any good-natured guy would do, which was to escort a drunk lady to her abode, thus Lauren was seen entering *Smallwood Plaza Apartments* where her unit was located.

However, things started to get a little suspicious when a passerby named Zach Oakes saw Cory and Lauren struggling to walk. Naturally, Zach asked if Lauren was okay because she was obviously intoxicated with alcohol; allegedly, Cory answered: "She's okay, I got it." but Zach, as if in an attempt to make sure that everything would be ok for Lauren, reiterated that he (Cory) should bring her back to her room.

Cory didn't like that sort of reprimand, so an altercation happened between the two, which ended up in Zach having to punch Cory causing the latter to fall head-first to the ground. Later on, Cory would claim that because of the blow, he lost his memory of that evening.

It seemed like Zach Oakes had reason to worry because at 2:42 am, Cory and Lauren were seen *exiting* the apartment complex. It wasn't clear why they went there in the first place, seeing that they only stayed there for a good 12 minutes, and the better portion of that time was spent in the fight between Zach and Cory.

One witness even saw Lauren sitting at the staircase, and due to her drunkenness, her head fell back with a loud thump on the concrete step. The witness approached them asking if Lauren was alright, and for the second time that night, Cory Rossman answered that he 'had it', that Lauren was alright.

Down the street, the couple walked until Lauren, in her

inebriation, fell down face-first -- she wasn't even able to use her hands to protect herself. Cory helped her up, guiding her, but then she fell for a second and third time. After that, Cory decided to carry her. By 2:48 AM, Lauren was seen entering an alley between Morton Street and College Avenue; three minutes later, she exited it, leaving behind her purse and keys. The CCTV record then showed her at a vacant lot.

But things were about to get vaguer.

It was seen that Cory took Lauren to his apartment, where his roommate, Michael Beth, helped them. At this point, it became evident that Cory, too, was drunk, to the extent that he vomited on the carpet. After escorting Cory to his bed, he offered for Lauren to stay the night, but the inebriated teenager refused, insisting that she wanted to return to her apartment.

The CCTV footage ended there.

At 3:30 am, Michael Beth claimed that he phoned Jay Rosenbaum, telling him to take care of Lauren. Apparently, Michael escorted Lauren up to Jay's place because the drunken girl was trying to drink again and even had the gall to invite Michael. Jay admitted that Lauren went to his apartment, and that he even observed that she had a huge black eye, presumably from the fall she took after leaving her complex.

While at Jay's, Lauren placed two calls-- one was to David Rohn, and the second was to another male friend. Neither of the two returned the call and they said that no messages were left to their voice inbox.

At 4:30 AM, Lauren allegedly left Jay's apartment unit; she was last seen at the intersection of College Avenue and 11th Street, wearing a white shirt and black leggings, with no shoes on. A few hours later, Jesse Wolff texted Lauren, but it was a person from *Kilroy's* who responded, informing him that the cellphone was left there by the owner.

Then, Lauren was reported missing by Jesse himself.

The Speculations

Lauren's case had everything, from drama to action, and of course to mystery. As sad as it was, her parents believed her to be dead, especially with the way she moved as seen in the CCTV footage: for them, someone must have mixed drugs in their daughter's drink.

Charlene and Robert were also open in their suspicion with the boys who had last seen Lauren. They were also suspicious of Jesse, even though he didn't seem to be present in any of the night's events. Apparently, they asked the men (Cory, Michael, Jay, David and Jesse) to undergo police-guided polygraph tests, but all of them refused.

Cory even insisted that what the Spierers were doing was harassment, and that they had been ruining his career. In his exact words, Cory Rossman said: "It is inappropriate the way they were harassing people who were also victims in this case. We've done nothing wrong. If we did, we would have already been arrested. All they're doing is hurting my career."

Additionally, the men countered that they had already undergone lie-detector tests, only, what they had were privately-issued because they did not trust the Bloomington Police.

All the men involved in the case, particularly Jesse and Cory, turned the tables on the alleged slipping of drugs. According to them, Lauren was a drug user-- an allegation backed by some of Lauren's friends. Nadine Wolff, Jesse's mother, even mentioned that Lauren was asked to leave the summer camp where she met her son and the others because of her drug use; she also added: "This poor little girl is not with us today because of her drug abuse."

However, if those drug abuse allegations about Lauren

were true, what does it have to do with her disappearance? Bo Dietl, the private investigator hired by the Spierer family, said that pot, cocaine, and pills were common-- they were not something that would cause one to go missing.

Whether it was slipped or was intentionally taken, the drugs (if it truly was in Lauren's system) could really have killed her. Alcohol mixed with drugs is dangerous enough, but more so if taken by a 90-lb girl who had a heart condition, Long QT syndrome. Long QT syndrome delays the heart's repolarization, causing irregular heartbeats.

If Lauren had died, where is her body?

Actions

On August of 2011, a 9 day search was done in Sycamore Ridge Landfill in Pimento, Indiana, but it led to nothing.

Charlene and Robert also filed a civil lawsuit (negligence) against Cory, Michael, and Jay, but the charge against Michael Beth was immediately dismissed based on the premise that he did help Lauren by escorting her to Jay Rosenbaum's apartment. The judge said that punishing Michael would dissuade others from helping people who are lost or sick because they face the possibility of a lawsuit should someone decide that the help they have offered wasn't enough.

Later on, the charges against Jay and Cory were also dismissed because of the lack of proof that their negligence could truly have led to Lauren's disappearance or death.

The grieving parents were disappointed, but they countered that "Disappointment does not mean defeat."

Hope

Despite the lack of progress, there's still hope for Lauren. Just April of this year (2015), the Bloomington Police investigated another angle which states that Lauren's case might be related to the disappearance and death of another IU student, Hannah Wilson.

Hannah, after spending time at *Kilroy's Sports Bar*, rode in a taxi and disappeared. Afterwards, her body was recovered in Brown County, Indiana. A man named Daniel Messel had been arrested after police determined that the cellphone lying near the body belonged to him. Despite the similarities, BO Dietl thinks that the two cases were not related.

As of now, Former FBI Agent Brad Garret is examining Lauren's case as a part of ABC's investigative series, *Solve*

It. According to him, the amount of time that had passed positively matters in the sense that people (who were involved) are now probably willing to speak, especially through social media. At this point, Brad is only collecting information, but he admitted that "a handful of them hold great potential".

So perhaps, we'll hear more about Lauren Spierer's case in the future.

Chapter 10: Taken by Her Non-Existent Grandmother

Erica Parsons had a life different from other children; unfortunately, it seemed like this difference cost her nothing less than her own life.

On March 2000, Carolyn Parsons, ex-wife to Steve Parsons, decided to put up her 2 year old daughter, Erica, for adoption. Knowing the life that could be brought by the foster care system, Carolyn realized that her only choice was to have her daughter adopted by none other than her ex-husband's brother, Sandy, and his wife, Casey. But don't be confused, Steve was not Erica's biological father; it was Billy Goodman, whose family *allegedly* resided in Asheville, North Carolina.

Not counting Erica, Sandy and Casey also had 5 biological children, one of whom was William "James" Parsons. It was him who reported the disappearance of his adoptive sister.

The Missing Persons Report

On July 30, 2013, 19 year old James Parsons was having a bad day: he had a fight with his parents and now, they were asking him to move out. Out of anger, concern, and confusion, he asked his parents (as he had countless times before) where his adoptive sister, Erica, was. Sandy and Casey insisted (like they had before) that she was with her birth relatives in Ashville. James was suspicious about the claim because his attempts to look for Erica in Ashville bore no fruit.

Out of anger, concern, and confusion, he went to the police to report the disappearance of 15 year old Erica Parsons.

In his account, James said that he had last seen Erica on November 19, 2011, just after they had moved to their house in Miller Chapel Road in Salisbury, North Carolina. In addition to the missing persons report, James also said that his parents could have been abusing his sister, although he admitted that he saw none of the abuse-- he only heard the neighbors talking about it.

Given the strangeness of the situation, the police immediately began their investigation.

Suspicious Parents

Since James reported the abuse and his suspicions about his parents, the authorities centered their attention to Sandy and Casey Parsons.

The couple began their "story" by reporting that in 2011, Carolyn, Erica's biological mother, contacted them, presumably to re-connect with her daughter. Since then, they allowed Erica to visit her biological father's family in Ashville three times. After the third visit in 2012, Sandy and Casey told the police that Erica had called them, telling them that she wouldn't be coming back-- that she would permanently be residing with her grandmother, Irene "Nan" Goodman.

But Carolyn knew none of this; in fact, she was adamant that the story was false. First and foremost, she knew nothing about any Goodman residing in Ashville; she insisted that Erica had no relatives in that area. The police did their own investigation and found out, from Billy himself, that his mother's name was Cloie, not Irene; furthermore, Cloie was long dead-- she was since 2005.

So, what were Sandy and Casey talking about? They even detailed the facts of the first meeting, which happened in September 2011 at a *McDonald's* branch in Mooresville, North Carolina. The next happened in December of the same year, and the last was in February of 2012, which was shortly after Erica's 14th birthday. It was then that Erica allegedly made the phone call, informing Casey that she would not be coming back.

If only Irene Goodman was a real person, it could have

given the parents an alibi to not look for Erica, but since Irene's existence is still in question, their reasoning was frowned upon. According to them, they didn't think to see how Erica was doing because they figured that she would be safe where she was at.

But where was Erica exactly?

Ulterior Motive?

Things got a little hazier when the police determined that Casey and Sandy were still cashing the checks from North Carolina Department of Social Services worth $600 per month. This was despite the fact that Erica was no longer under their care; they reasoned that they kept on taking it because they wanted to keep Erica's health insurance.

Could the parents purposely have "abandoned" Erica somewhere so that they could get the money in full amount? Authorities said that Sandy and Casey were uncooperative and they refused to give information unless a lawyer was with them. They insisted that James only reported the abuse and the disappearance out of spite, because he was being asked to move out.

The DSS found no evidence of abuse, but because of calls from neighbors, they decided to take the Parsons' two youngest children and place them under the care of relatives. After a couple of court hearings, the judge decided that they would only get custody back once Erica was found.

Has Erica been accidentally killed?

Many of Erica's extended relatives believe her to be dead; whether it was intentional or accidental, they were not sure. First of all, her death could be accidental as a consequence of the abuse. They insisted that Erica was small for her age, and on the rare occasions that they saw her, she always had bruises and bumps on her body.

They added that even when Erica was already 6 years old, she still wore toddler sized dresses and clothes. Aside from being shy and isolated, she also appeared fearful. Perhaps in the middle of the abuse she suffered, she was accidentally killed.

Or maybe, the couple killed her intentionally out of spite? Interview accounts from relatives indicate that the parents, especially Casey, detested Erica so much that at one point, she (Erica) had to stay with one of the relatives, Robin Ashely, because Casey didn't want to care for her any more.

The adoptive parent even admitted that she "didn't like Erica, couldn't stand to look at her, and didn't consider her to be her daughter." When Erica stayed with her other relatives, she began to gain weight, but just months later, Casey took her back in the fear that the adoption support money would also stop once the DSS noticed that Erica wasn't staying with them any more.

Imprisoned

In July of 2014, the Parsons couple was accosted with 76 charges including fraud, conspiracy, and theft of funds. Apparently, since Erica was last seen in November of 2011, the couple had already taken at least $12,000 in adoption assistance funds; they had also enlisted Erica as a part of their household when applying for benefits, and they had included her in their dependents list for tax exemption.

Casey pleaded guilty of 16 charges (some reports said it was only 15), while Sandy was found guilty on all of them. The judge believed that Casey was truly the mind behind all the offenses, hence, her verdict was to serve 10 years in prison, while Sandy was to be jailed for 8 years.

Little Hope

Erica's disappearance was lost in the radar for two

reasons: first she was isolated-- people saw her but not always, creating the illusion that if she wasn't seen, then it was alright. Second, she was home-schooled; there were no teachers, classmates, or concerned parents to report if something went amiss. Erica was totally on her own.

The judge who decided the verdict for the Parsons also said that he neither saw nor noticed any evidence that might indicate that Erica was still alive. However, if she is truly dead, then finding the body would be the least those people who sincerely loved her could achieve.

Conclusion

Thank you again for purchasing this book!

In this world that we live in, it is important to always look behind you. It is also imperative to look out for children because they are vulnerable and trusting.

One night in the bar can lead you astray leaving your wife behind with all the unanswered questions. It is important to make certain that the people around you can be trusted. If you trust the wrong person, they could take you away and never bring you back even when your mother is dying and you have a daughter behind.

While half of the cases featured here are old-- the other half are still current. The cases of Alyssa, Brooke, and Maura are still fresh, even though some happened more than a decade ago. The police are still investigating their cases. The important reminder here is for us to be vigilant-- who knows, perhaps in our everyday routine we will encounter a missing person?

If you enjoyed this book, do you think you could leave me a review on Amazon? Just search for this title and my name on Amazon to find it. Thank you so much, it is very much appreciated!

Check Out My Other Books

Below you'll find some of my other popular books that are popular on Amazon and Kindle as well. You can visit my author page on Amazon to see other work done by me. (Ryan Gillmore).

JFK Assassination

Missing People

Cold Cases True Crime

Unexplained Disappearances

True Ghost Stories

Cannibal Killers

You can simply search for these titles on the Amazon website with my name to find them.

Want more books?

Would you love books delivered straight to your inbox every week?

Free?

How about non-fiction books on all kinds of subjects?

We send out e-books to our loyal subscribers every week to download and enjoy!

All you have to do is join! It's so easy!

Just visit the link below to sign up and then wait for your books to arrive!

www.LibraryBugs.com

Enjoy :)

www.ingramcontent.com/pod-product-compliance
Lightning Source LLC
Chambersburg PA
CBHW050431290526
45786CB00003B/1477

* 9 7 8 1 5 3 2 7 9 5 3 7 4 *